ZERO TO SIX FIGURES STRATEGY

How to figure out entrepreneurship and make it work!

How to become a successful entrepreneur!

How to create satisfactory wealth!

TABLE OF CONTENTS

MONEY MATTERS

Chapter 1
MONEY MATTERS

"Money isn't everything, but its right up there with oxygen." — *Zig Ziglar*

Before you arrive at the point of developing and maintaining wealth, I will like to talk about a very important topic that you need to understand; and that is Money. This topic is not discussed as often as it should be discussed. Inadequate discussion is the reason why many people do not have enough money. The idea of enough

MONEY MATTERS

money depends on the individual. Those who claim they do not really care much about money are among those who do not have much on them and are almost always broke. The idea of not having enough money can make one feel hopeless and stressed up. I know what it feels like to also have enough money to spend and I have successfully created streams of income myself. Many who discuss topics related to money, income and wealth usually discuss these topics negatively. As a result, I will not be surprised if some people do not like the content or title of this book. There is nothing bad in being wealthy and becoming a millionaire. There is nothing bad in making all the money you can ever make in the world.

One of my past experiments showed that money brings a lot of excitement, fulfillment and enjoyment; it also gives me the opportunity to make choices. With the abundance of money, I can easily reach and spread to any limit and reach more audience. "Poor doesn't make any sense", according to Mark Daniel, my friend. If you still think being poor is ok, you need to get rid of that mindset. "If you're born poor, it's not your mistake. But if you die poor, it is your mistake," according to Bill Gates.

- "Has someone said any of these to your hearing?
MONEY MATTERS

- "Rich people are greedy set of people."
- "Money is the root of all evil."
- "Money will not make you happy."
- "You don't want to be one of those people."

Those lacking financial intelligence and freedom are usually found saying those words. Money, while being a great servant, can also be a bad master. You will not be able to build a lifestyle and also make your own rules if your only driving force is money. You must, therefore, find a way to make money and also live on your own terms, and I am here to guide you on how to do that.

One may easily get carried away by the stress of daily activities and overlook the ideas of prosperity, abundance and vision. Inability to meet daily needs tends to make building wealth more of an impossible task. Being consistently broke can also kill the idea of building wealth. These are issues at the front burner in the society of today. You need to overhaul your perspective about wealth and also have a clear understanding of how to create wealth if you must break free from mediocrity. This is not just about habits and actions; it is more about creating the right mindset

MONEY MATTERS

required for success. The book you are about reading will provide all the answers required for creating wealth. The content will change your perspective and habits toward helping you to create wealth.

Michael Jones, after years of studying wealth, has made some serious discoveries according to him; people in the world can be divided into four groups:

- **3% of people are wealthy:** they have up to $2 million assets, rich in assets, but poor in liquid cash. They have $2 million to invest

- **27% of people are comfortable financially:** They have a successful business or have a stable job. They either have a manageable mortgage or own a house outrightly. Such individuals can buy a car without getting a loan. Such individuals can stop working without becoming poor by the time they return back to work. Either you or your wife can stop working and still live comfortably.

- **55% are living from one paycheck to another:** it is easy to attain this classification. All you need to do is to spend more than you are making by putting more expenses on your credit cards and spending money on things that have no impact on the future. Such individuals will never advance financially. If you cannot skip a couple of paychecks without going broke, then you belong to this group. Such individuals are usually debt-slaves or have many kids that cause them to spend a lot of money from month to month. Members of this group will rarely be investing in themselves.

- **15% are serious debtors:** These individuals, aside from living from one paycheck to another, are also into debts. Up to 70% are accumulating debts monthly, aside from living from one paycheck to another.

I plan to push you to the top 30%. Also, understanding how to get there at a younger age will help you to get there faster. Money is not what will solve the problem. Those who think money will solve problems will have a really rough ride in life. What solves problem and creates wealth is intelligence. Problems can also be solved by personal growth. Money without financial intelligence is money soon gone.

MONEY MATTERS

ZERO TO SIX-FIGURES STRATEGY

It is my plan to be real with you and to also set you on the path to proper expectations. If you are making $10 per hour, you will need to work 29 hours per day for 365 days to make a 6-figure income. It is obviously not possible to work for 29 hours per day. If, on the other hand, you tend to be making $20 per day, you will have to work for 14.5 hours per day for 365 days to make your first 6-figures income. You can also make that 6-figure income by working for $48 per hour for 40 hours per week without going on a vacation.

This book is put together for individuals having the mindset of an entrepreneur, desire to become an entrepreneur or desire to create an amazing lifestyle for themselves. An entrepreneur is an individual that controls his income and use his implementations, ideas, relationships and intelligence to make money. An entrepreneur is not in the business of playing safe but ready to take risks. Examples of entrepreneurs are coaches, authors, speakers, leaders, business owners, network marketers and sales professionals, including every individual working for himself. Is it possible to be an employee and also be an entrepreneur on the side? Yes, it is possible. Virtually everyone will work as an entrepreneur at one point or another.

MONEY MATTERS

You will need four things before you can build a wonderful future for yourself and also get satisfied with what you do. If your business meets the criteria, then you are in the right spot. You should make corrections if your business does not meet the criteria. Loving what you do, building a satisfactory legacy and lifestyle is far more important than income. However, you need income to bring these to reality. The 4Ws to Lifestyle Satisfaction, according to Victor Stone, are described below:

The 3Ws for Lifestyle Satisfaction

- **What you do?:** What are the possibilities? Does it have endless opportunity? Do you enjoy doing it? Does it help and inspire others? Do you control your income, schedule and advancement? Most people claim they love what they do, but they will switch over to something else if they have the opportunity. If you love what you do, you will never see it as work.

- **What you do with what you do?:** Who are those leading you? How inspiring and challenging are they? I have been able to thrive in my endeavors because of the leaders and mentors that guide me; these mentors are living my desired lifestyle, having my desired kind of relationship and practicing what they preach. How much do you love your daily associates? Many people hate their co-workers, hate their boss and also hate what they do. Life is too short to have toxic people around you how flexible is your schedule? Can it be designed to fit around your preferred lifestyle? No one else controls your future except you and you can take it to any extent you want. However, you need to develop real passion so that you can attain your potentials. Are you up from bed long before the alarm sounds out of excitement or you are too unwilling to get out of bed? Gary Vaynerchuk said, "if you hate what you do, even a small percentage, it's time for a change."

- **Where do you do what you do?:** Can you work while on a journey or from home? Can you change your location if you so desire? Is your environment inspiring enough to spark your ingenuity and creativity?

If you hate to struggle financially or you want to increase how much money you are making, you are not alone. There are

MONEY MATTERS

only 24 hours in a day. Those who are thriving financially must be doing something very different with their time. Their perspectives about money and how to earn it must be different from those of others. I will give you some helpful tips to change your story if your income is not satisfactory.

- **Quit what you are doing:** You should stop what you are doing if you are not satisfied with it since it creates the reality you are currently facing. Albert Einstein said "Insanity is doing the same thing over and over and expecting a different result." what makes life great is the chance to change our stories and direction overnight. Irrespective of any past decision you have made, you only need one decision to make the right one.

- **Don't allow money to define you:** There is no link between your finance and your self-worth. You should never lose your confidence irrespective of your poor bank account. Even the stress you undergo should boost your confidence and motivate you to want to change the negative narrative. Being broke or being wealthy is a state of the mind. It is not what you have, but who you are that defines you.

ZERO TO SIX-FIGURES STRATEGY

- **Begin to prioritize your profits:** Always start your weekly schedule with activities that produce income. 20% of your activities account for 80% of your income. Find out about those activities and commit more time to them. Give some thought to the top three things you do to create more wealth and add them to your schedule on a regular basis; this will give you more assurance of creating wealth. You should also focus less on what you feel than what you do. Bear in mind always that impact drives income.

- **Commence the placement of a higher value on your time:** Time is recognized as having more value than money. You cannot get more time, but you can get more money. It is possible to make twice as much money and also become more valuable within the same limited period of time. Wise investment of time is the most valuable thing on earth. What you do with your 24 hours per day is what determines the result you get out of the day.

- **It is time and right to say NO:** The word is a life changer. If you are committing yourself to many things or overextending yourself, you can start saying no to certain things, especially those things that do not bring income to you. Continue doing this until your income has reached a secure and confident level. You can even forfeit tension-reducing activities for income-producing activities. "It's what Apple said 'NO' to that ultimately made them successful," said Steve Jobs.

- **Proximity to higher caliber of people is power:** Hanging out with broke people can also make you broke. It is time to start relating with people of higher caliber. You will find their attitudes, their ways of beings and belief systems contagious.

- **Lessen your excuses:** The bank account goes down as your excuses go up. The "Validators" OR excuse makers have the smallest bank accounts. Rather than wasting your time creating and giving excuses, you should utilize your time thinking of solutions to the issues and problems that will help you to move forward. Excuses are a disease and those who continue making them will continue to have money issues.

- **Push your focus away from victim to leader:** You should stop blaming your boss, your past, or the economy. You should also stop thinking that the world is working against you. Be ready to charge more for your services, become more valuable and switch jobs.

"The time you accept responsibility for each and everything in your life, is the time you can change anything in your life," according to James Ham.

Fast implementation makes the difference between ordinary and extraordinary income. How long will it take you to start implementing those plans for income increase? The content of this book will help you to create a higher level of income within just a few months if you take it seriously. Your bank account does not determine who you are; rather, it is who you were before changing your financial situation.

Chapter 2
UNKNOWN WAYS OF ACHIEVING WEALTH IN YOUR 20S AND 30S

Everyone wishes he can become wealthy. Some of us have the dream of becoming self-made millionaires in the future even if there are no pieces of evidence of that possibility such presently. However, you do not have to put your hopes into 'someday" to become wealthy. No one is ever too old to start out on the path to wealth. However, those who start building wealth from their young ages have more potentials and more time to become rich than someone that starts late.

Life is full of challenges in the 20s and 30s. For example, you may be faced by several unknowns, like a tedious career, student debt and several other challenges; these factors may prevent you from building wealth as fast as you desire. The path to wealth is not straightforward. However, the seven strategies discussed below can be of help in wealth-building while you are still young.

1. Put an end to procrastination

Procrastination involves believing that there is still time to achieve anything and this is common among youngsters. Many young people are of the opinion that wealth building or retirement plan will come later in life and, therefore, focus their attention on present concerns. However, procrastination always leads to future regrets. First of all, you must stop procrastinating. It can be scary to invest or save money. However, delaying will not augur well in the least.

2. Understand that there is no magic to wealth

There is no magical solution to wealth or the problems of life anywhere. The only solution to wealth building is to always make more money than you are spending. You can then invest the leftover very carefully and wisely. You can choose any investment you like, but make sure that the investment can bring the desired profit in the future. Make more money, spend less and invest wisely.

3. Spend more time and invest in yourself

Aside from the points above, you should also invest in yourself. You should spend more time and effort to educate yourself, refine your skills and venture out to associate with new people that may guide you towards achieving your life goals. The more connected, experienced, skilled and educated you are, the more opportunities you have in life. You can then get more pay and build a stronger financial foundation for yourself.

4. Carefully make a budget

It is important to make budgets so that you can know how to spend and what to spend on. The budget should be made based on your current expenses, income and the project to be completed. Make sure you place a firm restriction on what you spend and make sure you monitor where you have invested your money. You can then spend more time to refine your budget and then save or invest the remaining money.

5. Pay off all your debt

Before you start a regular investment and saving, make sure you pay off all your debts, like car loans, student debts and credit card debts that can accumulate heavy interest rates, which are capable to attracting monthly installment and pull you down financially. Leaving your debts unpaid can reduce your potentials. So, it is wise to make it your first-line priority to pay off your debts as quickly as possible.

6. Take risks and join the millionaires

You are young with the advantage of many years ahead of you. You, therefore, have more opportunities to take risks. Look out for higher- payoff, higher-risk stock opportunities. You can also think of quitting your job and starting a business. Never overlook new opportunities and new ventures. If things do not work out as planned, you still have enough time to recover. Most of the rich people around today took calculated risks, while the rest of the people prefer the safe route. You must, therefore, do things differently if you desire to break away from penury, even if those things are not comfortable.

7. Diversify your skills and investments

Risk taking has a great reward when you are in your 20s and 30s. Be that as it may, do not forget to diversify. Have different skill sets and build more professional connections. You should have more than one investment and avoid placing all your eggs in a basket in terms of investment. You should try to set up multiple streams of income and have several backup plans for your businesses and goals. Always be on the lookout for new opportunities. It will protect you from catastrophic losses and also make it easier for you to strike it big.

Putting the seven secrets above into consideration will help you to accumulate wealth faster, irrespective of your current situation in life. The first steps are not easy, like paying your debts, creating credentials, starting investments and so on. However, starting out early will bring massive financial success your way soon.

UNKNOWN WAYS OF ACHIEVING WEALTH IN YOUR 20S AND 30S

Chapter 3
ZERO TO SIX-FIGURES STRATEGY

" "**S**uccess rewards implementation, not knowledge"

I started my first entrepreneurial venture when I was 15 after being introduced to eBay. However, I could not make anything out of it until I turned 20, and this was because I was not doing anything worthwhile or challenging

ZERO TO SIX-FIGURES STRATEGY

with the knowledge I got. I was employed by a direct sales company and worked as an independent sales representative. I was, therefore, responsible for my own scheduling, customer base building and motivation. This gave me autonomy completely. I later realized how difficult it can be to create my own schedule and motivate myself. I was forced to invest in consistent improvement, but I was not used to it. Seeing people between the ages of 24 and 25 owning several homes and loving what they did was one of the factors that motivated me. I desired what they had and I knew this would make my life fulfilling.

I put in more effort at my work and became the District Manager less than nine months of being employed by the company. My rise was about the fastest the company had ever recorded in its sixty years of existence. As the District Manager, I was in charge of building my own sales organization and I had the freedom to build it as big as I want. I never knew being an entrepreneur was so challenging. I also realized that it is easier to motivate myself than to motivate others. I was ready to give up after just two months; the accompanying challenges made me thought being an entrepreneur might not be the thing for me. The misery and depression that accompanied these feelings were heart-rending. My savings were also depleting very fast. Then I got scared of losing control over my future, disappointing others and lacking the ability to buy the next meal were enough motivations for me. At times, I would sit down on my bed and wonder at what I did wrong and why I was where I was.

I was reduced to just two options:

Option number 1: Give up entrepreneurship

This option beckons on me to quit the ambitions, goals and dreams that I already have for myself. It also tells me to apply for an average job that will not be so demanding. Then I realized that quitting my goals then would turn me to a habitual quitter and I may find myself also quitting when the next challenge comes my way.

Option number 2: Figure things out and make them work

This option changed my life for the better. It teaches me to figure things out instead of quitting entrepreneurship. I then gave myself to personal achievements, business and development. I made up my mind to keep at it and get a good result out of it. I wanted to be my own boss so that I would not become like the 71% that got disengaged from work or the 69% still employed but bedeviled by a constant financial issue at 65. Kelly Vic shared a quote with me that changed my life:

"If you want to become a millionaire, talk to billionaires, you'll get there quicker."

I made up my mind to shun everyone that does not have my desired results around me. I only concentrated on those that are making waves in my preferred industry. A smart person would learn from his mistake, but those who are smarter and operate at world class level learn from the mistakes of other people, which will shorten their learning curve as it will reduce how much time they waste before achieving their desired goals.

ZERO TO SIX-FIGURES STRATEGY

You never know how strong you are until being strong is the only option you have. I am going to share the story of my journey with you to save you from making the kinds of mistakes I made. In fact, I would have killed someone if I could have this blueprint when I started off. This would have saved me so much struggle and pain. Everything I have written here is out as simple as possible and can help to change your perspective about wealth and also act as a guide towards achieving your desired goals and ambitions in life. I will be showing you the exact strategies and tools that I applied and still continue to apply, tools that have successfully created for me great results. You can apply these strategies and tools in virtually any industry or area of human endeavor and its applicability is not limited by your level of experience in your industry. Let us check out the six core principles. This book is highly interactive and you can find a helpful exercise in the last chapter. The need for progress is one of our biggest motivations in life as humans. "Progress is the ultimate motivation," according to Nelson Martin.

Concentrate on the chapter below and focus your mind on implementation and mastery. Also, do not forget to take action consistently and carry out the exercises here with intention and focus.

The 6 Musts from Zero to Six figures are highlighted below:

1. Total Clarity

2. Boosting Your Confidence Account

3. Moving Your Circle of Influence

4. Constant Energy and Motivation (Inner Drive)

5. Building Intentional Result Rituals

6. Consistently Focusing on Growth and Learning

I took time to reflect back to those low periods of my life and I realized that I didn't take full responsibility for anything during those years. Instead, I was playing the victim and blaming everyone, except myself, including my location, lack of resources, my company and the economy. I had a jaded focus and that put me where I was then. There was a need to change my intentions, perspective, attitude and myself. My life became simple and not complex anymore after I realized the above. At this point, I realized how much clarity can be powerful. I also realized that I needed to have a crystal clear idea of who I am and what I want if I wanted to achieve my desired results. I also became more motivated consequent of clarity. Be that as it may, I knew I had to take full responsibility for my current situation before I could change it for the better. I learnt to "adopt minimalism" from Robin Sharma. I also discovered that minimalism is one of the best ways to run a business and run one's life it helps to remove the noise and messes.

Obsession is the hallmark of genius: it does not help to try too many things at a time. One should rather be obsessed by few things capable of moving one's life and business forward.

You will start having interesting experiences when you gain clarity. For example, it will boost your confidence. Lack of confidence will make you record a consistent loss. Everything a man can achieve has its foundation in confidence in himself and his ability to "make it happen." The bigger the goals, the bigger the challenges. You will start seeing obstacles from the moment you make up your mind to go for your goals. The obstacles are there to put your faith and character to the test. They will also help determine if you are really serious or not about those goals that you have set for yourself. You will always win if you are consistently confident. The only security one can have these days is the security in one's confidence and ability to get results. John Maxwell once said:

ZERO TO SIX-FIGURES STRATEGY

"It's not what you do when you're on top that makes you a great leader; it's what you do when you are on the bottom that determines your leadership ability."

I was then forced to rethink my Circle of Influence since the personal associate will contribute to who I become. I detested becoming like the people around me and I took steps to link up with individuals that have recorded the kinds of success I want. The concept seems simple, but it made a really big difference in my business and performance. I realized that this is about the best way to become one of the top 5% in my industry. It is unfortunate that most people ignore this concept. I advise that you spend more time with the top performers in your industry since you will act and become those you associate with. Their ways of being, their attitudes and their belief systems will automatically rub off on you. My results and standards changed for the better after upgrading my peer group.

I could see other entrepreneurs get excited about new achievements and goals, but they lacked consistency. So, I made up my mind to be consistent and it made me more competitive in my endeavors. I discovered that lack of consistency can steal desires and dreams, though it does so subtly. It is important to improve your mindset consistently. You must also improve your philosophy, perspective and emotional intelligence on how you view yourself and how to achieve success. You shouldn't only do things when you feel like it, but keep at it even when you do not feel like working on it. This will give you more momentum than ever in your business. When I started seeing progress, my mind begins to grow and I felt even more consistent motivation and energy. Nothing brings more confidence and energy than progressing towards your goal.

When you maintain consistency for long, you can easily determine the strategies that work and differentiate them from those that do not work, and you will see the pattern rising. It will help you to detect where the desired results are coming from so that you can create Result Rituals that will help push your business towards your goal. Action will always get you and your business out of any rot or problem. At the same time, you must be intentional and strategic. I was committing between 60 and 80 hours a week to work without getting many results. However, the trend changed after I could detect those result rituals capable of moving my

ZERO TO SIX-FIGURES STRATEGY

business forward. After making this discovery, it was easy to organize my daily schedules around those priorities and actions.

How can you consistently record new heights in your business and life? Just continue to grow and learn more and also continue to become the best at anything you do. This is about the main reason why 95% of people are not operating at a higher level in their business or life.   You will find out that they stop growing after reaching a particular level. However, that is exactly where learning really starts.

Before I further dissect the six tactics, I want to show you the most dangerous words concerning success and learning. Examples of such words are "I already know that," and "Yeah, I've heard that." So many businesses, income opportunities, dreams and goals have died consequent of those words. You need to consider the questions below:

• Am I doing the right thing? Have I gotten it mastered?

• Does my waistline show I have gotten the right thing mastered?

• Does my wallet show that I have gotten the right thing mastered?

ZERO TO SIX-FIGURES STRATEGY

- Does my business success currently show I've it mastered?
- Do my relationships show I have them mastered?
- Does my daily attitude and perspective show that I have all these principles mastered?

If you answer "no" to any of the questions, then you need to master some areas and improve further. Once you are aware of the areas you need to master and develop, it will then be easy to create an action plan that you can take action on. The results you can get from this can be lasting and transformational.

Chapter 4
THE GREATEST MONEY-MAKING AND WEALTH CREATION SECRET IN HISTORY!

You are only required to do one thing if you want money.

This is one thing many of the wealthiest people on earth have done and are still doing.

Several ancient cultures have also written about this one thing and are still promoting it today.

WEALTH CREATION SECRET

It can bring you money if you do it, but it is being ignored by many people today out of fear.

What is that one thing?

It was done by Jon D. Rockefeller when he was a child and it turned him to a billionaire.

It was also done by Andrew Carnaige and he too became a tycoon

What is this great secret to making money in history?

 What is this secret that can be applied by anybody?

Give out money.

Yes, you heard me right. Give money away.

Give it out to those individuals that can help you to remain in touch with your inner world.

Give it to those who love you, heal you, serve you and inspire you.

Give money out without expecting the receivers to give it back to you, but with a full understanding that the money will return to you in many folds from other sources.

John D. Rockefeller in 1924 wrote a letter to his son in which he showed his son how to practice giving money away. He writes in the letter, "... at the beginning of getting money,

WEALTH CREATION SECRET

away back in my childhood, I began giving it away, and continued increasing the gifts as the income increased..."

He gave more money away as his income increased. In his entire lifetime, he gave away a total of $550 million.

Some people were of the opinion that Rockefeller was doing a publicity stunt to improve his public image when he was giving money away. This is far from the truth. Ivy Lee was a public relations person working for Rockefeller. A biography of Ivy Lee titled Courtier to the Crowd; Ray Eldon Hiebert said Rockefeller had been involved in giving money away for many decades on his own.

Ivy Lee was only saddled with the responsibility of informing the public about it.

Another person that gave a lot of money away was P.T. Barnum. In one of my books, I wrote about him saying, "There's A Customer Born Every Minute, Barnum believed in what he called 'profitable philanthropy'" he is fully aware that he will receive more when he gives money away. As a result of his consistent giving, he became one of the richest men on earth.

WEALTH CREATION SECRET

ZERO TO SIX-FIGURES STRATEGY

Andrew Carneige is yet another person that applied this principle of giving money away. Consequently, he joined the league of the richest men in the history of America.

Bruce Barton co-founded the famous BBDO advertising agency; I made him the key subject of The Seven Lost Secrets of Success, another of my books. He also believed in the principle of giving to receive. He wrote the following in 1927: If a man practices doing things for other people until it becomes so much a habit that he is unconscious of it, all the good forces of the universe line up behind him and whatever he undertakes to do.

Consequently, Barton became a best-selling author, very wealthy, contributor to innumerable causes, and business celebrity.

You may want to argue that the individual mentioned above had enough money to give away, which made it easy for them; however, you must also consider the fact that they could make so much money because of their willingness to give money away freely. Their giving made it possible for them to receive and led to more wealth for them.

WEALTH CREATION SECRET

ZERO TO SIX-FIGURES STRATEGY

Bear this in mind that: The giving led to the receiving.

You will get more wealth when you give.

Many businesses find it fashionable these days to give for worthy causes. Such an action improves the public image of these businesses aside from helping them to receive more. Some of the examples of companies that give and receive are Patagonia belonging to Yvon Chouinard, Ice Cream belonging to Jerry Greenfield and Bwen Cohen and Body Shop Stores belonging to Anit Roddick

My focus here is on individual giving. My focus is on you giving out money so that you can receive money.

One mistake many make while giving money is that they give too little money. They prefer to hold on to a large chunk of their money and only give in trickles. Such individuals are, therefore, not receiving. You must be ready to give a lot so that you can receive a lot.

I never agreed with the idea of giving when I first learned about this concept. I thought it was a ploy to collect money from me.

WEALTH CREATION SECRET

ZERO TO SIX-FIGURES STRATEGY

Even if I ever gave in those days, I gave miserly. The things I got in return were in the same measure that I gave.

Then I made up my mind one day to test out this theory about giving

I could encourage myself to give via the inspirational stories I read about giving.

My thanks go to www.fabsocialmediaassistant.com for sharing inspiring messages with me and several others through email. Then I made up my mind to give him some money. I would give him five dollars in the past, but I had the fear that the principle may not work. Then I decided to change my strategy and wrote a check of one thousand dollars for him.

This was about the largest single contribution I have ever made up to that time in my life.

I was somewhat nervous after giving such a huge amount of money. However, I could not forget about the excitement that followed. I was so excited to be rewarding Vic.

And I also wanted to see if anything positive would happen.

WEALTH CREATION SECRET

ZERO TO SIX-FIGURES STRATEGY

Needless to say, Vic was more than surprised. He was so excited that he almost drove himself out of the road after getting my check. It was simply too big for him to believe. He later called and thanked me for the gift. His gratitude made me feel like some millionaire.

I never bothered about what he decided to do with the money; I just gave it to him delightfully and with the satisfaction that it made him happy. I got this wonderful feeling of being of help to someone else in his good works. And until today, I am still happy to send him money.

Then I started experiencing certain wonderful things.

Then someone called me to co-author his book. I got some much money from this project several times more than I had ever earned. Later, I was contacted by a publisher in Korea, who wanted to purchase the translation rights to Home Culture, my bestselling book.

I was also paid several times more than the gift I gave to Vic

If you are skeptical, you may say there are no relationships between these events. They may not be so in your skeptic mind, but they are so in my mind.

WEALTH CREATION SECRET

ZERO TO SIX-FIGURES STRATEGY

Giving money to Vic announced me to myself and the world around me that I was a prosperous person and this brought the inflow. I also successfully set up a magnetic principle that could attract money to me: what you give is what you get. If you give time you will get time. If you give money, you will get money.

You will get products if you give products
You will get love if you give love
You will get money if you give money

Your finance can be transformed by this one tip have you found anyone that had inspirited you recently; someone that has impacted your goals, dreams, life and existence?

Give money to that person. Give it to them form the depth of your heart. Avoid being stingy. Give abundantly and not scantily. You should also give without ever expecting them to give you back.

Your own prosperity will show up as you give.

This is about the greatest secret to money making.

"If you see it, touch it.

If you touch it, feel it.

WEALTH CREATION SECRET

ZERO TO SIX-FIGURES STRATEGY

If you feel it, love it.

If you love it...Give it."

Giving speaks to the universe louder than anything else about your belief in love, abundance and self than giving.

Once the universe hears about your giving, it will automatically cause more to be added unto you.

I hereby challenge you!

"If it doesn't challenge you, it won't change you"

— David Tom

WEALTH CREATION SECRET

ZERO TO SIX-FIGURES STRATEGY

The only two things that are capable of changing your business and personal life are:

- Something new coming from inside you
- Something good or bad coming into your life

It may take time to wait for something good to come into your life. Bear in mind that you do not have the time to wait. Instead of waiting, you can simply look for something inside you. It is hoped that this book has changed your mindset about giving scanty talents and gifts so that you can start enjoying life better. If you find anyone getting more from life than you, it is a sign that the person is amplifying himself better. However, you can put an end to this.

You should never count the life-changing capability of this book. We will take a 30-day challenge and you must be totally committed to it if you must get the desired positive change in your finances. If you give your all to this program, you will be ion a dominating position and will never be hampered by bad economy. Commitment and total dedication can bring anything you want your way.

WEALTH CREATION SECRET

ZERO TO SIX-FIGURES STRATEGY

You will go on money making vacation for the next thirty days. Everything will automatically change for you when you change. You must be primed about your ambition and be ready to become that person that you must become before you can achieve the dreams. It is complete insanity to expect a different result when you do not change your strategy.

People in the world are classified into two. Those who are set to do anything they have to do to create wealth or their dreams. The second group includes everyone else. It is left for you to choose which group you want to belong to.

Chapter 5
THE ONE MONTH CHALLENGE

Today's Date:_________________ Goal Date:

____

What are your top 5 goals you wish to achieve within the next 30 days?

1.____

2.____

3.____

4.____

5.____

THE ONE MONTH CHALLENGE

ZERO TO SIX-FIGURES STRATEGY

Give a breakdown of your weekly task to make sure you achieve your 30-day goals.

Week 1 Top 3:

1. ____

2. ____

3. ____

Week 1 Reward: _______________________

Week 2 Top 3:

1. ____

2. ____

3. ____

Week 2 Reward: _______________________

Week 3 Top 3:

THE ONE MONTH CHALLENGE

ZERO TO SIX-FIGURES STRATEGY

1. ____

2. ____

3. ____

Week 3 Reward: _______________________

Week 4 Top 3:

1. ____

2. ____

3. ____

Week 4 Reward: _______________________

Immediately your 30 days challenge gets over, how are you going to feel? It's vital for you to look deeply with precision the feelings you're going to get when the 30 day challenge ends.

____

______

____

______

____

______

____

THE ONE MONTH CHALLENGE

ZERO TO SIX-FIGURES STRATEGY

____

____

____

____

____

____

Commencing Today:

Highlight the key behaviors required to achieve your 30-days goals'?

1. _______________________________________

2. _______________________________________

3. _______________________________________

Do you have any weekly rituals that must occur no matter what? If yes, state?

1. _______________________________________

2. _______________________________________

3. _______________________________________

THE ONE MONTH CHALLENGE

ZERO TO SIX-FIGURES STRATEGY

What's your today's activity that's in line with your 30 day challenge goals?

____

____

____

____

____

What do you require to put an end today that's not in line with your 'Big 5', keeping you back, or putting an end to your current progress or momentum?

____

____

____

____

____

What do you intend to continue doing that's been of great service to you?

THE ONE MONTH CHALLENGE

ZERO TO SIX-FIGURES STRATEGY

____

____

____

____

Signature ____________________ Date

____

ZERO TO SIX-FIGURES STRATEGY

You should take these things very seriously and also act more intentionally in your endeavors. There is a certainty that you will get the desired freedom, lifestyle and wealth if you work at them. If you want to live an inspiring life, express your creative genius and live your potential, then you should never leave the tips provided above out of your daily activities. You can achieve anything in life if you put your mind to it. However, you must be ready to make the sacrifice and take the right actions.

If you are one of those taking 100% responsibility for your wellbeing, this is about the best time for you. If you commit to these activities that your life deserves and you engrave it into your mind, you will always be in control of your economic situation at all times, irrespective of the prevailing circumstances.

I'm here for you, and once you complete this 30-day challenge, please share your success story personally with me at Support@fabsocialmediaassistant.com.

Aid in spreading the word about the Zero to Six Figures Strategy and stay connected: Follow me on Twitter @ https://twitter.com/fabVAssistant and friend me on Facebook @ https://web.facebook.com/fabsocialmediaassistant/.

THE ONE MONTH CHALLENGE

ZERO TO SIX-FIGURES STRATEGY

I love to connect with great minds like you.

As I thank you for purchasing Zero to Six Strategy and committing yourself to excellence, building a business that matters, and taking control of your future, I've assembled a series of valuable tools you can use to help maximize your entrepreneurial experience. Stay in touch via the above social media platforms and you will surely get yours as soon as the tools are readily available.

THE ONE MONTH CHALLENGE

ZERO TO SIX-FIGURES STRATEGY

Brubarer, K.P. "wealth creation, Poverty Reduction and Social Justice: A world council of churches perspective" International conference on Religion and Globalisation. Chiang Mai, Thailand July 27 – August 2, 2003.

Stackhouse, M.L., McCann D.P., Roes, S.J., Williams, P.N. (eds.) On Moral Business, classical and contemporary Resources for Ethics and Economic life. Grand Rapids, MI: Eerdmans.

Enderle, E. Business Ethics and wealth creation: Is there a catholic Deficit? ¾ Landes, D.S. 1999. The wealth and poverty of nations: why some are so rich and some are so poor. New York: Norton.

World Bank. 2000. Can Africa Claim the 21st Century? Washington, D.C 18 ¾ World Commission on Environment and Development (WCED) 1987. Our Common future. New York: Oxford University Press.

THE ONE MONTH CHALLENGE

Mwakapui, A. A reflection account on the possibilities of achieving reduction in poverty in the context of low levels of economic growth and underdevelopment democracy and good governance-working group three in Development Policy Management Network Bulletin Vol. IX. No 1, February 2002, pp. 36-38

Tonge, A., Greer, L., Lawton, A. 2003. The Enron story: You can fool some of the people some of the time ---- Business Ethics: A European Review, 12/1, 4-22.

UN Report prepared for the June 2000 World Summit for Social Development Session. ¾ Vedder, R.K and Gallaway, L.E. 2001. Wealth and Poverty Revisited (accessed from http://www.house.gov/jec)

www.fabsocialmediaassistant.com